Watching Clouds

Gerry Boland

DOGHOUSE

Watching Clouds

is published by
DOGHOUSE
P.O. Box 312
Tralee G.P.O.
Co. Kerry
Ireland
TEL: +353 (0)66 7137547
www.doghousebooks.ie
email: doghouse312@eircom.net

ISBN 978-0-9565280-5-6

Edited for DOGHOUSE by Noel King

Cover illustration: Evening Mist, by Roscommon artist, Sue Hill (1952-2009)

The publisher and poet thank Roscommon County Council for its financial support towards this publication.

Further copies available at €12, postage free, from the above address, cheques etc. payable to DOGHOUSE also PAYPAL - www.paypal.com to doghousepaypal@eircom.net

Doghouse is a non-profit taking company, aiming to publish the best of literary works by Irish or Irish resident writers. Donations are welcome and will be acknowledged on this page.

For our 2011 publications, many thanks to

Kerry Education Service

Printed by Tralee Printing Works, Monavalley Industrial Estate, Tralee, Co. Kerry

Contents

watching clouds

I'm a long way from café society
floating somewhere between
dreamtime and the clouds
drifting in from the east

I no longer need the tonic
of an office to run or a meeting to chair
nothing from another life that kept me
up and running from espresso to espresso

I can cook a damn fine meal
suspend time on an old armchair
and if the phone ever rang
I suspect I could handle the crisis

mostly though I am what I am –
adrift beneath a frame of stars
lost to the moon's mystery way up there
in the middle of my rooftop window

once I could take a call with two already holding
run off a few letters at the drop of a hat
now I reflect on the beauty of clouds
make small talk with the spiders

the consultant's waiting room

gone

the Spring chorus rising
from the birchwood beneath my house
the muscular sea swell
down at the Forty Foot
the whisper of soft kisses in the dark
those rare nights you stayed over

and there's the peculiar loss of silence
of meeting it on a lonely lane
when the wind dies in mid-afternoon
and I can hear only
the soft landing of my sneakers on the dry earth –
now when I stand still I no longer hear

the frantic beating of my heart

from here to New York

a familiar breeze returns
it carries from the west
memories of a day that dissolved
into myth, into vapour

today I am clearheaded

awake to the warm gusts
blowing across the valley
the speckled butterfly settled
on a lingering wildflower
the frenzied fly
obsessing at my feet
the huddle of unpicked blackberries
beyond the gate

a sense of a sudden surge of activity
among small things
as they inch towards their own apocalypse

September 11, 2003

impulse

there's something not quite right
about suddenly wanting to stab your lover
the impulse comes at perverse moments
while Ella sings, a fire glows and candles flicker
and your lover reads beneath the lamp
curled up cosy on the sofa
you made love on an hour ago

you would never do it, could never do it,
yet you panic, overwhelmed by a wild desire
that comes from nowhere –
you know in your silence that
nowhere does not exist
that impulses come from somewhere

you stand at the kitchen counter
you have no idea who you are

the way it is

you are the only person I can be myself with
my mother got the same treatment
got it in the teeth
took it like a loving mother

but you
you are tiring of my petulance
the sheer impossibility of me
and rightly so in my opinion

unlike my long-suffering mother
who took it on the chin
you will not stand for it
you will throw it back at me

it will land like dry spit on parched skin
as you turn your back
in the age-old way
of strong women and weak men

terstown Strand

e same dogs chase the air
till duped by the unthrown stick trick
worms weave installations in the sand
an ancient daily tradition
long slender fragile shells
crunch beneath a walker's feet

lovesick couples will paddle
in shallow channels that teem
with tiny fish and baby crabs
until the sea recedes forever

for now
continue to be fooled by the notion
you could walk from here
across the wide expanse of sand to Howth

imagine
there's a child on the strand
with a yellow bucket and spade

my father's voice comes to me now
bidding *good day* to perfect strangers
striking up conversations about the tide
the weather, the famous Booterstown cloud
that hangs above and hides the sun
from dawn till dusk

but look
if he was here now he would take a wide berth
of this pair of boyos now bearing down on me

twilight and I am all alone here

on being a man

there's a rumour doing the rounds
that I am not a man

it's true that men I know
can erect a polytunnel in a day
cobble a stove together
from spare odds and ends
take a car engine apart
put it back together

other men I know
can wire an entire building
knock up a tree house
between breakfast and lunch
lay a stock-proof fence single-handedly
figure out how the world works
by simple observation

I am bereft of manly skills
can do none of these things

I am not remotely bothered by any of this
I remain cool and calm inside this knowledge
in what you might call an emotion-free zone

I am it would seem a man after all

room service

I am more than happy
to haul your luggage
on and off trains and buses
through airports the size of small cities
up treacherous stairs in budget hotels

be my guest dear
pack for six days
when we're going for two
for a month
when we're going for a week

I am your intimate porter
your transportable lover
toss me on the bed
unzip and unpack me
whisper *room service* in my ear

thinking about transience

The Buddhists talk a lot about transience.
I can see their point. Recently I've noticed
nothing can be counted on not to change
or to leave altogether like you have, baby.

Now they want to axe the trees beside my house.
I'm programmed by all that has led me here
to stand at my door and smoke my peace pipe
and watch the trees keel over one by one

but your departure has short-circuited my wiring
(God knows what I've done with my peace pipe)
I need an army of tree-climbing monks
to colonise a dozen doomed specimens and chant

the whining chainsaws into silent submission
while I reflect on the pros and cons of change.
Renewal has its place, don't get me wrong
but right now I'd like things to stay as they are

while I catch my breath.

out to grass

yes, that is me you see over there
firmly wedded to the pavement
watching others go to battle

see how they agitate
chant banal slogans
build up a head of steam
bang heads against walls
in the age-old game
of guarding our freedom

I lost wars out there
tussled with men in suits
the frontline of no-win missions
points scored in petulant skirmishes
small pyrrhic victories that made
the heart beat a little faster

I stand stranded at this intersection
view the new recruits as they straggle past
keep an eye out for old war comrades

flip sides

each photo has its flip side

laughter before battle
singular days that were sweet and sour
darkness lurking in the sunshine

a brand new issue to be fought over
an old one unpacked, dusted down –
against the odds we would continue

to turn our love on its head

we're squabbling now

I act as your trigger
you act as mine
tiny sparks explode
like timeless bombs

we live in remote galaxies
you in yours
me in mine

and there's that coldness
you've encountered
or so you tell me
and who am I to argue

but I do anyway

I'll trample all those eggshells
you place at my feet
my clumsy feet
your fragile shells

repossession

here you are, finger on the bell
farewell speech rehearsed
everything about you now
points to a wicked determination
and though you do tentative well
I am not fooled
this is my house after all
that is my front door you point towards

and those are my footsteps
you can hear receding
as the door clicks shut
and you breathe in the silence

before turning to survey the debris

the cottage, Derreenadouglas

you'll barely recognise the place
I've spent all day preparing

the long grass cut down to size
a year's amassing of moss
shovelled and swept aside
those monotonous masonry blocks
revelling in their splashed whitewash
that pile of useless clutter
shifted and scorched
and in its place a makeshift rockery
pinned with wildflowers plucked
before the raging strimmer
dancing an ecstatic dance
to the winds of second chance

as we shelter in our long grass
longing for an unexpected Spring

blue

I will wake one soft Spring morning
to a call from an old friend
checking in on me, that I am, as he will say
still in the land of the living

over breakfast my sister will touch base
she will claim to be the bearer of good news
though there will be no news worth giving
and no news worth hearing

out of the blue an old flame will drop by
dipping her toe, testing the lie of the land

in the afternoon I will walk
through the bluebell wood below the house
by now lulled into a false belief
that the world is full of tenderness

like a bolt out of another blue
I will recall the wood we discovered last year
the bluebells we tried to count
the bark of the beech tree you had your back to

the way you pushed against me
and though I lost my faith a long time ago
I will pray for a crack team of loggers
to tear down every bluebell wood I know

orange

hurtling backwards towards a past or a future
the fields and hedgerows and lonesome houses
open up briefly before they fade into themselves

all the night creatures are lying low
cows flick their ears to a horn-blast, warning
of an incident that might or might not happen

we rumble past stranded whitethorn and ash
and meadows brushed flat by the wild westerlies
that have blown for six breathless days and nights

a German couple run out of things to say
at the end of a wet fortnight
a teenager sleeps, her soft red curls a cushion

on the cool glass that shields her from the storms
newspapers rustle and sigh
there is laughter at the far end of the carriage

a rank orange pulped into the fold-up drinks tray
is a shocking orange to the grey day
although clearly spent it flashes its essence

as if to prove it has plenty of living to do
before it relinquishes its identity
outside the hedges continue to rush by

ghost houses gaze glumly at our passing
swallows swoop and soar honing their skills
in preparation for another unimaginable journey

a cloud of starlings steal the borrowed light
and on an isolated hill above a flooded plain
a lone donkey rails against the injustice of it all

I stare at my reflection in the window
and my pale self stares back, mockingly,
as if my reflection is withholding information

that I do not wish to hear, at least not now
not this moment,
this unplanned for, unexpected moment

another summer

it has been another good summer
I have not mown down any children
old men or young mothers wheeling their buggies
I have not crushed the skull of a commuter
cycling home from work nor have I obliterated
an entire family returning from vacation

there were other fatalities that I should record –
on a dull grey day in May a robin
loitered too long on a road that led me home
others, blackbirds in the main, timed their wheel-
height bullet-flights with staggering ineptitude
white butterflies zigzagged
one last time on lazy afternoons
while moths in their hundreds fluttered blindly
from darkness to headlight to a permanent night

in recompense I became a petty saviour
seeking compensation and forgiveness
snails were moved out of danger zones
spiders gathered before a morning shower
drowning flies rescued and resuscitated
I entertained the notion of selling the car
but somehow knew that such a course of action
could only be construed as having gone too far

pig farm

a sow stands short-shackled
to a concrete floor decked with
shit-smelling piss-soaked wooden slats

she shifts and struggles
wrenches with sumo neck
an unbreakable chain
lurches in slow motion
against immovable bars

her agitation over
she settles back to standing still
slurps at an iron bar for absent minerals
waits for her session on the rape rack
a term the men use with an ugly smile

ten thousand live here, from
day-old piglets to sows worn out
by never-ending pregnancy

they lie wedged between bars
slumped on their colossal sides
while regiments of newborn piglets
suckle with clipped teeth

night patrol

what would my neighbours think
if they saw me on this empty road
tap unsuspecting snails into my palm
lob them gently into the long grass?

most mornings I come across
the mashed remains of those
who crossed the night-blue tarmacadam
on epic voyages of unlikely ambition

I often wonder are the dead those
I plucked from almost certain death
but in their slug-like stubbornness
took one last shot at crossing

that great hard divide to the other side
where the grass seems always greener

woodpigeon

you are an innocent in all this
no need to alter your plea
you remain in all eyes free of guilt

your song is exquisite
but the language of your soul is foreign
to those who make the rules

from midnight
they will seek you out
sinister figures who lurk

behind hedgerow and tree cover
crouch beneath dense shrub
slyly hide in a quiet hut

you will sense that they are there
you will burst out into your last sky
a single bullet will bring you down

first of the month
a fine bird that
good start to the season

0032

across a ragged fence like windblown lace
your silksoft ears wave bright yellow tags
nice to meet you 0032
you have a freshness about you

unlike your elders long settled
in their lazy languid lives
though your shorn horns
and your absent testicles

a truffle-treat perhaps for
the hungry farm dogs
testify to an early trauma
somewhere in these wet bogs

daft calf with your ridiculous ears
you stand stubbornly
against the improbability of human love
go now to your mother

go to her, sweet calf, while you still can

everyday things

now that you've told me
that belt I bought in Benalmadena
will remain where I've left it
coiled in a chest of drawers upstairs

now that you've told me
I cannot bring myself to unravel it
thread it through the waist loops
fasten the buckle I knew so well

now that you've told me
I see complicity everywhere
in bags and belts, wallets and hats
shoes and boots

cruelty in everyday things

thrush

you were in full fantastic flight
bristling with life
now you're a small brown parcel of softness
crumpled on this wet tarmac

did I do this?
your shattered leg
your broken neck
your miraculous wings stilled

I will never know
where you built your home
nor who you have left behind
condemned from this moment

when I pick you up
your head falls limp across my palm
your beak leaks a droplet of blood
dark as altar wine

three cuckoos

today must be the day
to lay an egg in a stranger's nest

I watch the exaggerated swooping of swifts
and swallows as a brutal bird strategy
unfolds in this quietest of valleys

up on the treetops it's guerrilla warfare
as three cuckoos cause havoc among
scrambled warblers and meadow pipits

go pick on a hooded crow, raven or rook
try bullying that lot with your hollow cacophony

my neck aches from twisting to see
the desperate measures you will go to
in laying your responsibility at another's door

conversations with snails

you need a quiet place
to begin with, to tune in
to their feint frequency

be still then and listen
as soon as you hear one
you will hear them all

their tiny voices
deeper than you might think
spiraling upwards

their curious conversation
and the range of topics they cover
on a slow afternoon

make them ideal companions –
I can hear them now
gathering in the dark

their other-worldly whispers
on the front doorstep
guiding my feet to safety

elephant song

there she is again
hanging about our grand piano
it's the ivory that draws her

the sadness of it
compelling her to tinkle-trinkle
on those bleak teeth

she's playing a lament
for her brothers and sisters
her great grey ancestors

what's surprising is
the delicacy of touch
the trunk softly landing

on our grand colonial piano

the visitor at the lion enclosure, Dublin Zoo

once a year he comes
to stand and stare
a ritual of sorts

for why else would he come
and linger so long
a lonesome soul

oozing melancholy
across the dead air
until even he can't stand it any more

the rest
the daily irksome circus
pass blindly by

unmoved by it all
I force myself to breathe
one long slow breath, then another

he is here now
completely still
I watch his sad eyes

mirrors of mine

death of an opportunist

the old gardener turns a sod
observes a familiar opportunist

pluck another hapless worm
from its upended world

decides he has turned enough earth
today and perhaps for a lifetime

he makes his way home
to chop some wood and light a stove

and isn't there to see the young sparrowhawk
new to her trade yet already

an old hand at snuffing out life
snatch out of the twilight a drowsy robin

on her way home after an easy day's feeding

spider

it was an exquisite embalmment

she whined like a cheap camera rewinding
ready for a precise delicious devouring

I could not watch
I could not look away
ran you from the crime scene
ground her out of her misery

while I'd cooked and while I ate
you had spun your web in silence

while I read and while I'd slept
you'd re-configured re-set re-spun
made minute adjustments
settled back to wait

your perfect stillness
death's reflection

stray

this time it was a flying ant
loitering on a leaf whose lettuce head
was bought and boxed and driven
five miles up the road

hours later my eyes are drawn
to a feeble fluttering of tiny wings
a disorientated stumbling
across my kitchen counter

and I know I have stepped
one more time into God's domain

easy here in the closeted anonymity
of a silent kitchen to take up the cause
of a small life in distress
oversee a quiet liberation

not so easy was the down-and-out dog
I came upon in Sligo last month –
I am haunted by that look you gave me
as I turned a blind eye

love

my stopping here outside your padlocked gate
an outrageous act of defiance
unleashes machine-gun barks
that would scatter a squad of rookie postmen

your ferocity soon crumbles
as I uncover a chink in your armour
that the balm of my smoothtalk
will enter and disarm

in a short while you will smother me
in shameless slobbering affection
betrayed by your species' singular failing
an incurable soft spot for humanity

Tyson – I will have to call you Tyson –
you are falling in love before my eyes
and it's clear that there is damn all
that you can do about it, my friend

a very tidy village

even the cows are tidy in Keadue
they lie in manicured meadows
a neat pastoral composition duly noted
by the Tidy Towns judges

it can't have been easy
persuading the beasts to toe the line
throw their considerable weight behind
the orderly local committee

no one knows why they came on board
cows care little for neatness
even less for personal hygiene
some say it was the perseverance

of the Tidy Animals Sub-Committee
who after Mass every Sunday
stood at the wall of the meadow
to offer a role model to the cows

who continued to chew the cud
on the face of it oblivious
to the curious human choreography
yet perhaps taking it all in slowly

as cows tend to do

drowning

drowning off a safe beach is not difficult
Atlantic waves, a retreating tide, a sharp
belt of a body board, and lifeguards
swimming to a false alarm a lifetime away

it's all over in minutes, though
it hasn't yet begun for your mother
who is happy you are happy, here
on this warm August afternoon

she looks up from her book
smiles expectantly, scans the sand
for her only child, sees a gathering
commotion at the water's edge

out of the corner of her eye

wild poppy

you look like you belong
in a gardener's garden

not pushing through cracks
in the concrete
of an abandoned farmyard
or emerging into lost spaces
swept by intercity expresses

your false fragility
is nature's way of saying
don't be fooled by appearances
there is room for whimsicality
in my evolutionary narrative
and besides
tenacity may wear a mask

you pioneer those barren places
that we have left for dead
your red flag petals a waving on
an unexpected warning
that all is not as it seems
that this is no place to linger

ONLY ROTTERS HUNT OTTERS

now that you're gone
all I can see is the jam-jar badge
you wore like a stop sign
on the collar of that fake fur
you slept in through our only winter

it was your passport
to a one-way conversation
or once
a hunting down of a rich bitch
until we snared her

in the doorway of Hackett's Shoe Shop –
she might have been my mother
frightened and cowering
inside her mothball mink
her eyes caught in your hungry glare

platform one, Pearse Station

that's the thrill of it
the freedom to do the unthinkable

shall we say tomorrow
between eleven and eleven-thirty

a leap into the unknown
from platform one, Pearse Station?

we didn't know, they will say
didn't he keep his troubles well hidden?

now that it's firmly in my mind
why bother putting it off?

a bread knife across the wrist
a kitchen devil thrust into the heart

that would do the trick
be almost as quick

still, all things considered
probably best to stick to plan A

platform one Pearse
does have a nice ring to it

poetic, alliterative
memorable

important points to consider
I think you'd agree

hands

he'd spent a lifetime keeping them warm
inside long forgotten pockets
on cold winter days and nights

on summits of countless mountains
he blew into their clenched tunnel
a funnel to capture warm breath

on bikes he rode into a hundred blizzards
unerringly they steered him home

some kind stranger picked them up
put them in a plastic bag she filled with ice
sent them off in a taxi to the hospital
they were an odd front seat passenger
the rest of the body gone ahead beneath
flashing lights and a siren screaming

he asked to take them home
for seeds sown and trees planted
for the zillion balls caught and thrown
for the greetings and the goodbyes
for the countless knots they tied
for skin touched and hair tousled

he asked to take them home
they were his hands after all
not a pretty sight they said
and besides
we're afraid we've lost them

he has no hands now
they were taken twice
once by a freak accident
later by incompetence
or perhaps at the end by stealth
grafted on to a rich amputee
who paid generously
for such a pair of gems

he wonders will he recognize them
if by some uncanny coincidence
they enter the room he is in –
he does little else these days but
stare at the hands of strangers
seeking out his lost jewels

the trouble with philanthropy

something odd is at work
in our central character
categorised a cold fish
by those who claim to know him

a disease of the emotions
passed down by a father
who could summon tears
at the drop of a Hollywood hat

he is on the point of blubber now
over someone he doesn't even know
some canny philanthropist
who gave all his money away

why should he care?
why *does* he care?
he knows none of the beneficiaries
who litter the book he reads

whatever it is it is spreading
its soft-centred sentimentality
to the point that he no longer knows
when the cynic slipped away

something odd is afoot and
must be kept at bay, must never
see itself reflected in the eyes
of those who claim to own him

commuter

five-twenty-five from Euston
forty minutes in
you nod off mid-crossword
drift into a recurring dream

in your dream an old gorilla
slouches and shuffles around
his barren enclosure, turns once
to stare through you at a face

at the window of a passing train
a face submissive and defeated
with eyes that yearn for a place
he will never reach

you wake with the usual shudder
to a crowded silent carriage
turn to the flat landscape
yawn at its dreary familiarity

costa

back home a nation is at work
no one seems to toil on this coastline
formed by fifty million years
of nature's endeavour

here was monumental work
by the relentless caress of the sea
it took fifty years to bury under
tower blocks and tarmacadam

sea of sameness
sea of flesh
a bounty
of bare breasts

look at how they walk
beasts of burden in the sun-haze
their sell-by date a melanomic mark
on withered skin

after a lifetime of struggle
under dark northern skies
it's from here they'll endeavour
to hold back the tide

college days

a fly nestles in the x of Stanley Baxter
carved on a wooden memorial bench
her diaphanous wings buffeted
by gusts of a thunderous June

nearby a wasp woodpecks along lines
of weathered varnish and a youthful
sparrow wingbeats to the rugby pitch
searching for worms caught offside

magpies strut their stuff before biology
crows perch like sentries on goalposts
campus bristles with end-of-term endeavour
while beyond the cricket pitch and over the wall

a restless city that no longer sleeps
murmuring insistently from morning to night

Sandra is heading to the capital

she's lost again, this eternally hopeful
thirty-something short-haired blonde
making the best of what God gave her

the men have taken over the conversation
one in particular
with his Seymour-Hoffman voice
his talk of Warhol and Pollock
of Columbia and MGM
a lecture on documentary film-making at its best

it's a steady stream of references and name
droppings and hard-won deals
agents and lawyers and getting the backing
blah-de-blah-de-blah

his captive, a slightly older man
with suave glasses and greying hair
who seemed reasonably content to go along
with the blonde's amiable chat
now reverts to type, defers to Mr Big opposite
in a refined New York accent
he asks the right questions
shows the appropriate level of interest

Sandra, I am calling her Sandra
has dropped her head in submission
has opened her new Maeve Binchy
has not read a single line since Mr Big got on
she hopes he will disembark at Maynooth
but frankly she doesn't hold out much hope
these guys are heading to the capital
where Mr Big will meet other Mr Bigs

Sandra too is heading to the capital
she will meet no one as she makes her way
via her local SuperValu
to her neat little box flat by the river
where she is guaranteed
to feel safe and lonely

a different economic perspective

the professor of economics keeps a clatter
of abandoned pots in his kitchen cupboard

some pour prodigiously, others ponderously
worst of them all the common stainless steel

with its chattering lid, its irrepressible gushing
leaves small black lakes on the table

porcelain is his true passion
always a steady fill, not a drop spilt

a pour of simple grace and purity
porcelain pots, he tells me over afternoon tea

can revive this ailing economy
and he showed me the paper he'd written

and sure enough, it all added up

end of the road

sooner or later you were bound to tire of me
now I've done the dirty
driven you against your spluttered reluctance
to Frank, once your healer
now a dealer in your spare parts

your mission is to motor
in death you are motionless
stripped down parts leaning
against a garage wall
awaiting an ailing recipient

your flaking body discarded
until a truck is summoned
to take you to your new life
a small heavy square of metal
reworked into something artistic

a city spire perhaps
useless and pointing at the sky

gardener's dream

you were in someone else's garden
digging weeding watering
your name was Parsley of all things
Rosemary daughter of Basil and Sorrel
sister to Marjoram and Camomile
all Parsleys from Mullingar
townies
big house long garden

you dreamed you had a visitor
Ginger dropping by
on his way to Beijing
your phone rang
it was a man named Dill
looking for Sage
wrong number

you woke when you opened a letter
from someone who signed themselves
Sweet Potato Butterhead

you showered
dressed
put the kettle on
went outside and cut enough fennel
for your morning infusion

the air was heavy with the odour of wild garlic

winding down

suddenly I seem to have got older
I wouldn't mind if I could pinpoint
a moment a date a period an event

then I could say yes
that was it now it makes sense
but no nothing like that

everything moves more slowly now
as if someone prised me open
in the middle of the night

removed a battery
perhaps even two
yet couldn't be arsed to tell me

give it to me straight whoever you are
is this how it's going to be from now on
a battery here a battery there

until my troubled heart gives out?

sapling

you do not know it but a day will come
when you are near your prime
reaching for the sky
and on a morning much like other mornings
men you've never seen will set out from a depot
and by noon you'll be sawn to a stump

that day your seed signalled its irrepressible intent
beneath power lines and telephone wires –
was that plain carelessness on your part
perhaps a rare case of arboreal suicide
or was it what I suspect
just one more example of nature not keeping up?

moon

a wizened ash cradles you
in her ancient branches

parcels of cloud provide
a frame of slow shadows

you rise
on the waters of the world

pull them towards you
push them away

a dog howls
planetary tides obey

Gerry Boland is originally from Dublin, and now lives in north Roscommon, where he works part-time in a community organic garden. He is a writer-in-residence with a number of schools in counties Roscommon, Sligo and Leitrim.

He has published two travel books on Dublin, the most recent being *Stroller's Guide to Dublin*, published by Gill & Macmillan in 1999. *Watching Clouds* is his debut collection. *A Rather Remarkable Grizzly Bear* (a children's illustrated trilogy) is due from O'Brien Press in 2011.

Also available from DOGHOUSE:

Heart of Kerry – an anthology of writing
from performers at Poet's Corner, Harty's Bar, Tralee 1992-
2003

Song of the Midnight Fox – Eileen Sheehan

Loose Head & Other Stories – Tommy Frank O'Connor

Both Sides Now - Peter Keane

Shadows Bloom / Scáthanna Faoi Bhláth – haiku by John
W. Sexton, translations, Gabriel Rosenstock

FINGERPRINTS (On Canvas) – Karen O'Connor

Vortex – John W. Sexton

Apples in Winter – Liam Aungier

The Waiting Room – Margaret Galvin

I Met a Man... Gabriel Rosenstock

The DOGHOUSE book of Ballad Poems

The Moon's Daughter – Marion Moynihan

Whales off the Coast of my Bed – Margaret O'Shea

PULSE – Writings on Sliabh Luachra – Tommy Frank
O'Connor

A Bone in my Throat – Catherine Ann Cullen

Morning at Mount Ring – Anatoly Kudryavitsky

Lifetimes – Folklore from Kerry

Kairos – Barbara Smith

Planting a Mouth – Hugh O'Donnell

Down the Sunlit Hall – Eileen Sheehan

New Room Windows – Gréagóir Ó Dúill

Every DOGHOUSE book costs €12, postage free, to anywhere in the world (& other known planets). Cheques, Postal Orders (or any legal method) payable to DOGHOUSE, also PAYPAL (www.paypal.com) to doghousepaypal@eircom.net

"Buy a full set of DOGHOUSE books, in time they will be collectors' items" - Gabriel Fitzmaurice, April 12, 2005.
DOGHOUSE
P.O. Box 312
Tralee G.P.O.
Tralee
Co. Kerry
Ireland
tel + 353 6671 37547
email doghouse312@eircom.net
www.doghousebooks.ie